POPULAR SONGS
HAL LEONARD STUDENT PIANO LIBRARY

Cool Pop

Arranged by Mona Rejino

T0057196

ISBN 978-1-70512-292-1

Visit Hal Leonard Online at
www.halleonard.com

Contact us:
Hal Leonard
7777 West Bluemound Road
Milwaukee, WI 53213
Email: info@halleonard.com

In Europe, contact:
Hal Leonard Europe Limited
42 Wigmore Street
Marylebone, London, W1U 2RN
Email: info@halleonardeurope.com

In Australia, contact:
Hal Leonard Australia Pty. Ltd.
4 Lentara Court
Cheltenham, Victoria, 3192 Australia
Email: info@halleonard.com.au

From the Arranger

Cool Pop showcases chart hits by some of today's most popular artists. Each song tells its own story, and the various themes include love, loss, memories, and aspirations. From tender ballads to driving Rock beats to Latin pop, you will find all sorts of moods to explore. May this music bring meaning to you and all who hear it performed.

Mona Rejino

———◦◦◦———

An accomplished pianist, clinician and teacher, **Mona Rejino** is co-author of the *Hal Leonard Student Piano Library* and *Adult Piano Method*. Her numerous published works in the Hal Leonard Piano catalogue include solos, collections of original compositions, arrangements, chamber music, and *Essential Elements Piano Theory*. She was commissioned by MTNA to write a trio for the 2019 National Conference and was named the 2021 TMTA Commissioned Composer. Mona has taught piano at the Hockaday School in Dallas for over twenty years.

CONTENTS

Blinding Lights

Words and Music by Abel Tesfaye,
Max Martin, Jason Quenneville,
Oscar Holter and Ahmad Balshe
Arranged by Mona Rejino

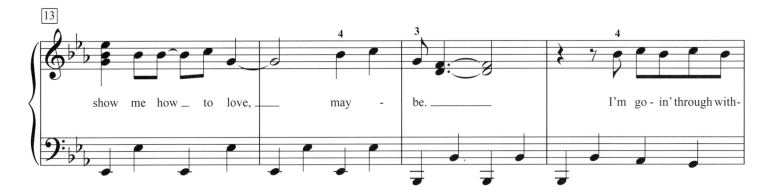

show me how to love, may - be. I'm go in' through with-

draw'ls.
time, 'cause I can see the sun light up the sky.
You don't e - ven have to do too much.

You can turn me on with just a touch, ba -
So I hit the road in o - ver - drive, ba -

by. I look a - round, but Sin Cit - y's cold
by. The cit - y's cold

and emp - ty.
and emp - ty.
(Ah.) No one's a - round to judge me.

5

(Ah.) I can't see clear - ly when you're _ go - o - one. I __ said,

ooh, _____ I'm __ blind - ed by __ the lights. __

__ No, I can't sleep __ un - til I feel __ your _____

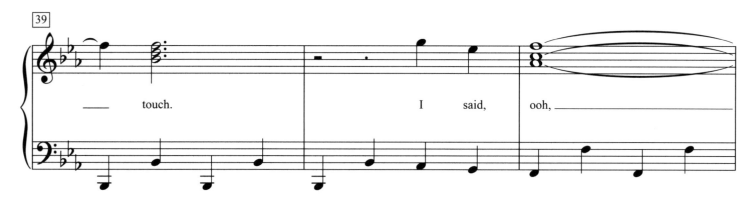

__ touch. I said, ooh, _____

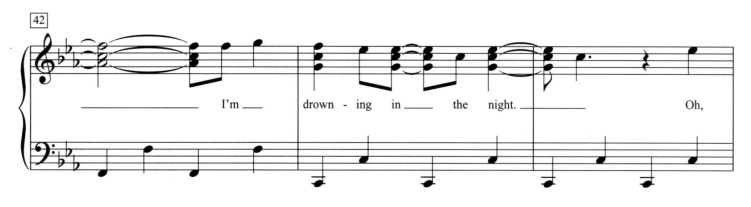

_____ I'm __ drown - ing in __ the night. _____ Oh,

6

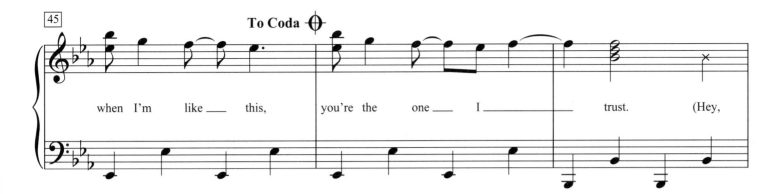

when I'm like this, you're the one I trust. (Hey,

hey, hey.)

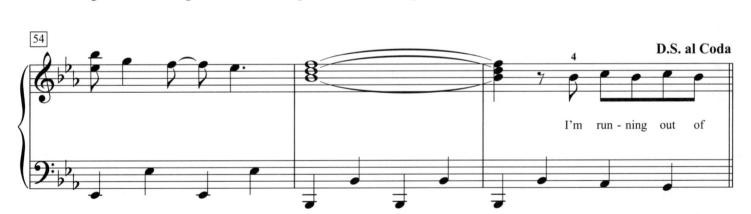

I'm run - ning out of

you're the one I trust. I'm just walk - in'

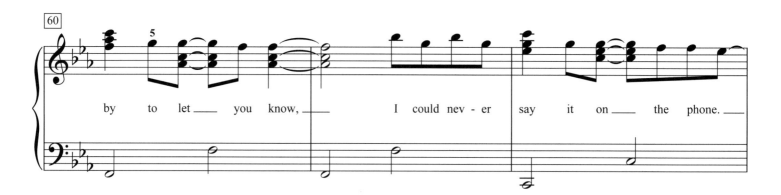

by to let ___ you know, ___ I could nev - er say it on ___ the phone. ___

_____ Will nev - er let ___ you go _____ this time. ___

_____ I said, ooh, _____ I'm ___

blind - ed by ___ the lights. _____ No, I can't sleep ___ un -

til I feel ___ your _____ touch. (Hey, hey, hey.)

(Hey,

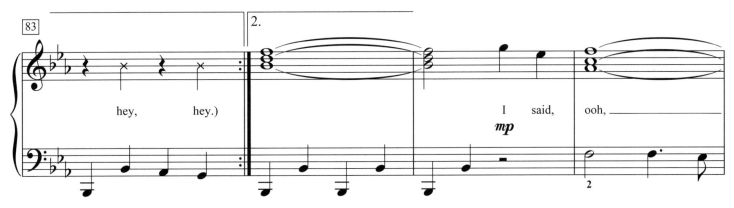

hey, hey.) I said, ooh, _____
mp

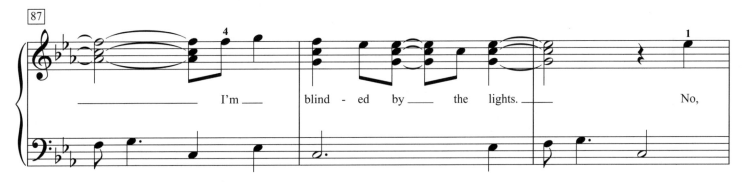

_____ I'm _ blind - ed by _ the lights. _____ No,

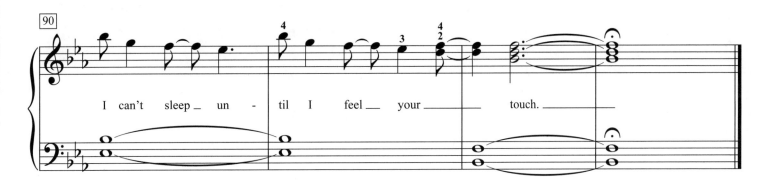

I can't sleep _ un - til I feel _ your _____ touch. _____

9

Cardigan

Words and Music by Taylor Swift
and Aaron Dessner
Arranged by Mona Rejino

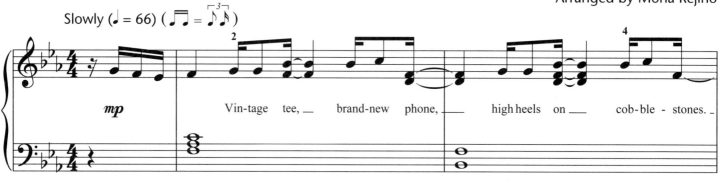

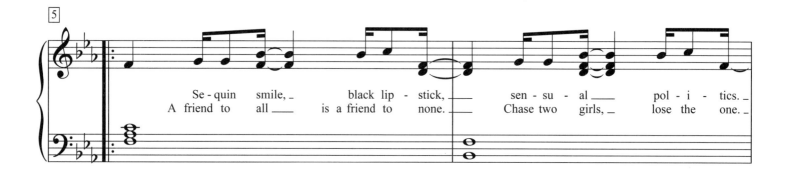

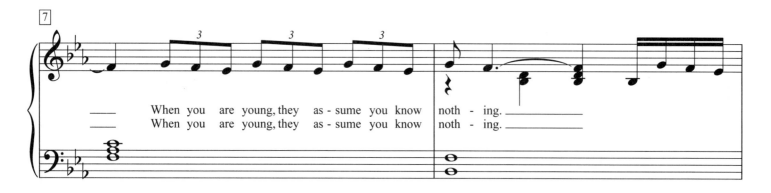

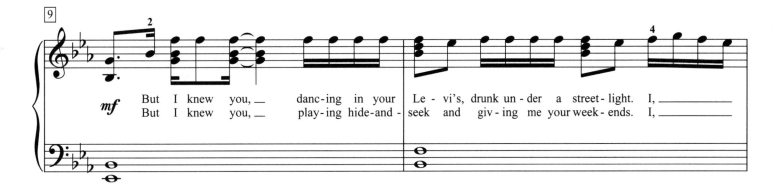

But I knew you, __ danc-ing in your Le - vi's, drunk un - der a street-light. I, __
But I knew you, __ play-ing hide-and - seek and giv - ing me your week - ends. I, __

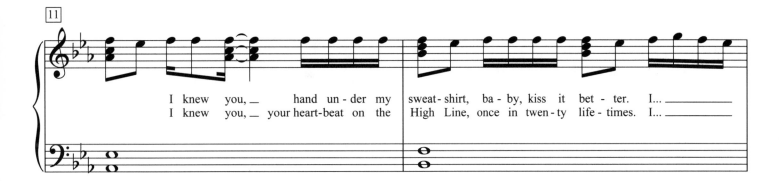

I knew you, __ hand un - der my sweat-shirt, ba - by, kiss it bet - ter. I... __
I knew you, __ your heart-beat on the High Line, once in twen-ty life - times. I... __

And when I felt like I was an old car - di - gan __ un - der some-one's bed, __
And when I felt like I was an old

you put me on and said I was your fa - v'rite. __

car - di - gan ____ un - der some-one's bed, ____ you put me on and said I was your

fa - v'rite.

To kiss in cars ____ and down-town bars ____ was all we need-

- ed. ____ You drew stars a-round my scars, ____ but now I'm bleed - ing. ____

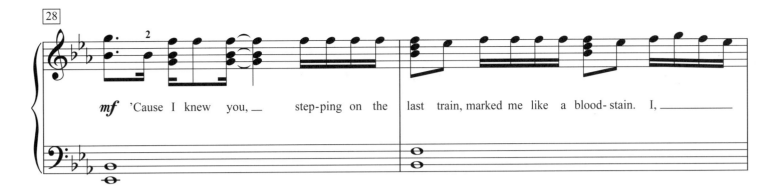

mf 'Cause I knew you, — step-ping on the last train, marked me like a blood-stain. I, —

I knew you, — tried to change the end - ing, Pe - ter los - ing Wen - dy. I, —

I knew you, — leav - ing like a fa - ther, run - ning like wa - ter. I... —

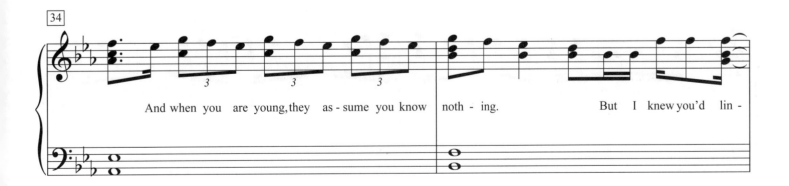

And when you are young, they as - sume you know noth - ing. But I knew you'd lin -

13

- ger like a tat-too kiss. __ I knew you'd haunt __ all of __ my "what ifs." __ The smell of smoke __

__ would hang a-round this long __ 'cause I knew ev - 'ry-thing when I was young. __ I knew I'd curse __

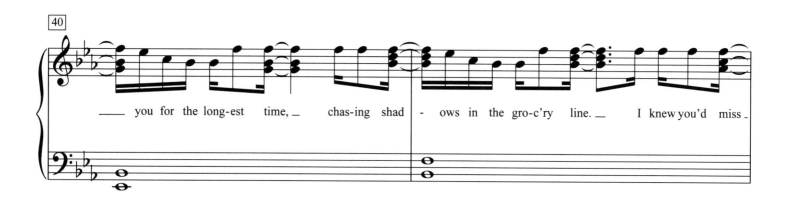

__ you for the long-est time, __ chas-ing shad - ows in the gro-c'ry line. __ I knew you'd miss __

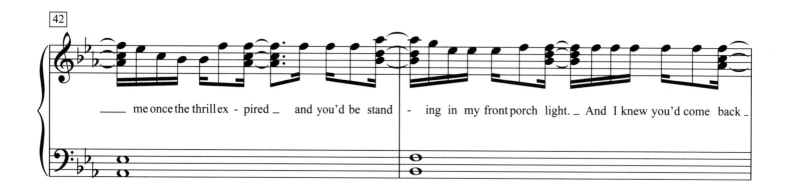

__ me once the thrill ex - pired __ and you'd be stand - ing in my front porch light. __ And I knew you'd come back __

14

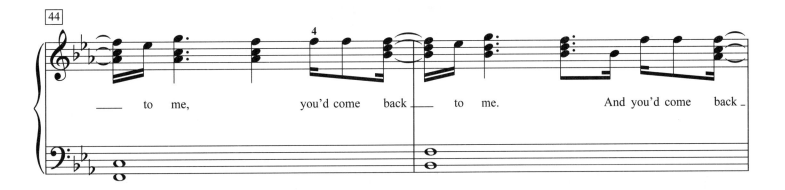

_____ to me, you'd come back _____ to me. And you'd come back _____

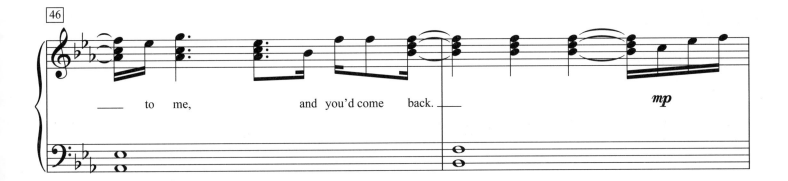

_____ to me, and you'd come back. _____ **mp**

And when I felt like I was an old car - di - gan _____ un - der some-one's bed, _____

you put me on and said I was your fa - v'rite.
rit.

High Hopes

Words and Music by Brendon Urie,
Samuel Hollander, William Lobban Bean,
Jonas Jeberg, Jacob Sinclair,
Jenny Owen Youngs, Ilsey Juber,
Lauren Pritchard and Tayla Parx
Arranged by Mona Rejino

With pedal

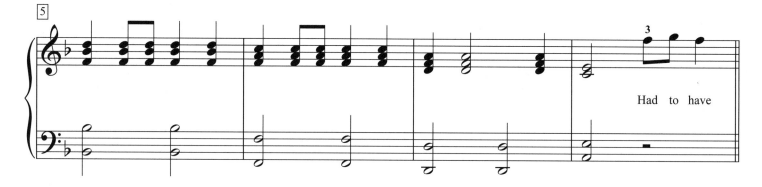

Had to have

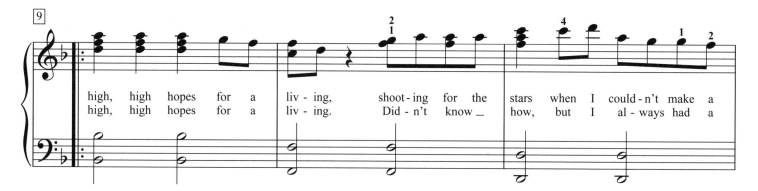

high, high hopes for a liv-ing, shoot-ing for the stars when I could-n't make a
high, high hopes for a liv-ing. Did-n't know _ how, but I al-ways had a

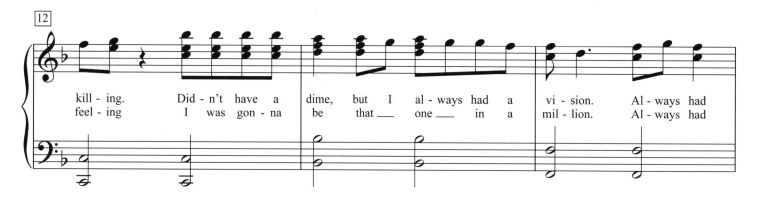

kill-ing. Did-n't have a dime, but I al-ways had a vi-sion. Al-ways had
feel-ing I was gon-na be that _ one _ in a mil-lion. Al-ways had

high, high hopes. — | Had to have
high, high hopes. — | Ma - ma said,

"Ful - fill the proph - e - cy. | Be some - thing great. — | Go make a leg - a - cy."

Man - i - fest des - ti - ny. | Back in the days, — we want - ed ev - 'ry - thing, want - ed

ev - 'ry - thing. | Ma - ma said, | "Burn your bi - o - graph - ies.

Re - write your his - to - ry. | Light up your wild - est dreams." | Mu - se - um vic - to - ries,

ev - er - y day.___ We want - ed ev - 'ry - thing, want - ed ev - 'ry - thing. Ma - ma said,___

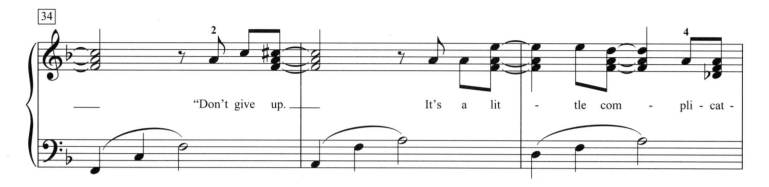

___ "Don't give up.___ It's a lit - tle com - pli - cat -

- ed. All tied up,___ no more love,___ and I'd hate___

___ to see___ you wait - ing." Had to have high, high hopes for a

liv - ing, shoot - ing for the stars when I could - n't make a kill - ing. Did - n't have a

18

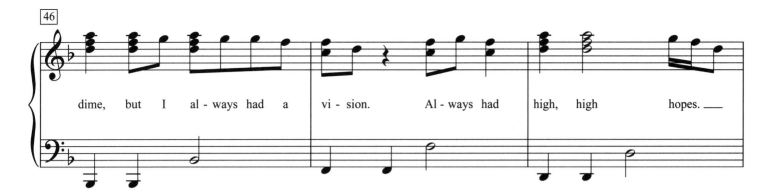

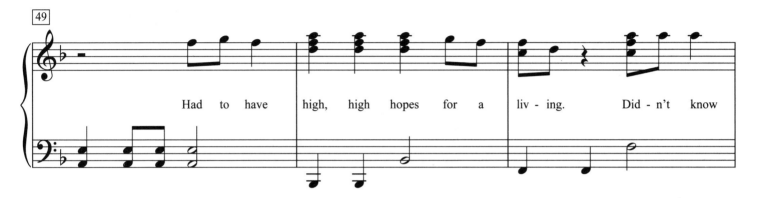

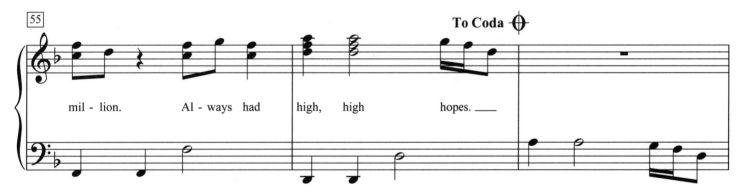

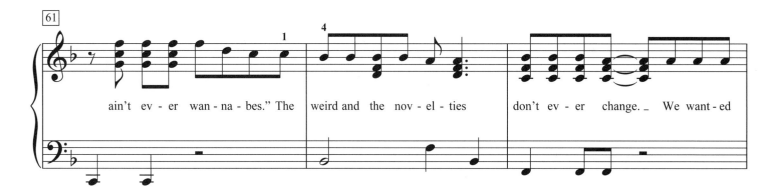

ain't ev-er wan-na-bes." The weird and the nov-el-ties don't ev-er change.__ We want-ed

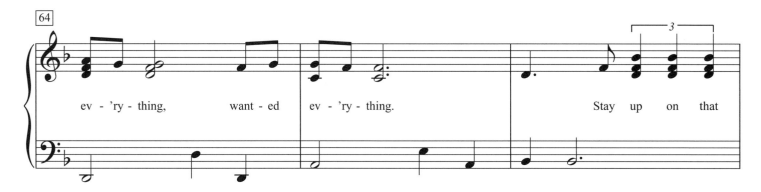

ev-'ry-thing, want-ed ev-'ry-thing. Stay up on that

rise, stay up on that rise and nev-er come down, oh.__

__ Stay up on that rise, stay up on that rise and nev-er come

down. Ma-ma said,__ "Don't give up.__ It's a lit-

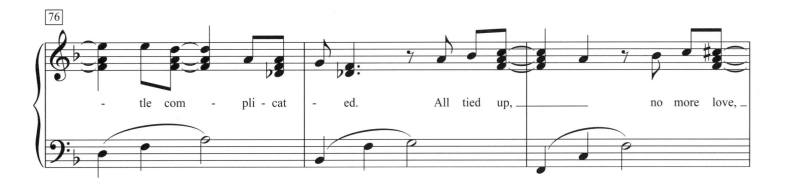

-tle com - pli - cat - ed. All tied up, _____ no more love, _____

_____ and I'd hate _____ to see _____ you wait - ing." They say it's

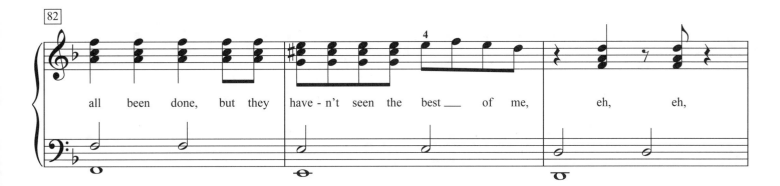

all been done, but they have-n't seen the best _____ of me, eh, eh,

eh. So I got one more run, and it's gon - na be a sight _____ to see,

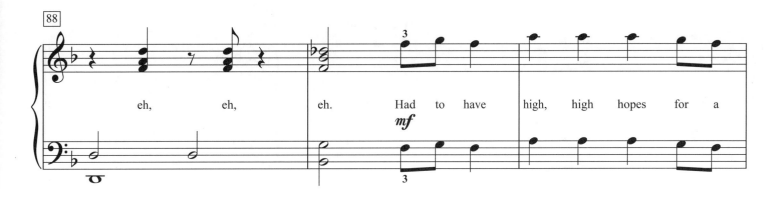

eh, eh, eh. Had to have high, high hopes for a

living, shooting for the stars when I could-n't make a kill - ing. Did-n't have a

dime, but I al-ways had a vi - sion. Al - ways had high, high hopes. ___

Had to have high, high hopes for a liv - ing, Did-n't know how, but I al-ways had a

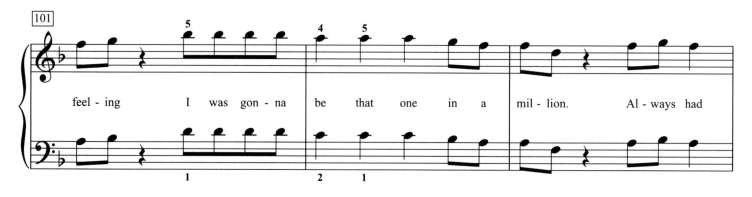

feel - ing I was gon - na be that one in a mil - lion. Al - ways had

high, high hopes. ___ Had to have

D.S. al Coda

CODA

22

Memories

Words and Music by Adam Levine,
Jonathan Bellion, Jordan Johnson,
Jacob Hindlin, Stefan Johnson,
Michael Pollack and Vincent Ford
Arranged by Mona Rejino

Relaxed groove ($\quarternote$ = 92)

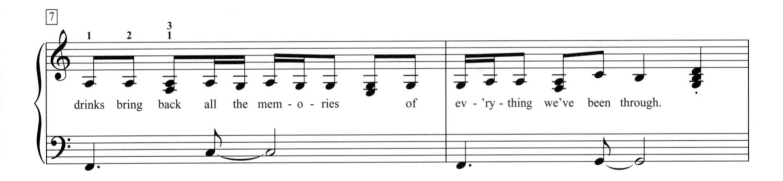

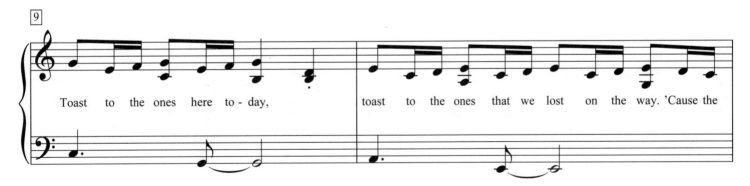

drinks bring back all the mem - o - ries, and the mem - o - ries bring back, mem - o - ries bring back

you. There's a
time that I ____ re-mem - ber when I did not know ____ no pain, ____ when I
time that I ____ re-mem - ber when I nev - er felt ____ so lost, ____ when I

be-lieved in ____ for - ev - er and ev - 'ry - thing would stay ____ the same. ____ Now my
felt all of ____ the ha - tred was too pow - er - ful ____ to stop. ____ Now my

heart feels like ____ De - cem - ber when some - bod - y say ____ your name, ____ 'cause I
heart feels like ____ an em - ber and it's light - ing up ____ the dark, ____ I'll car -

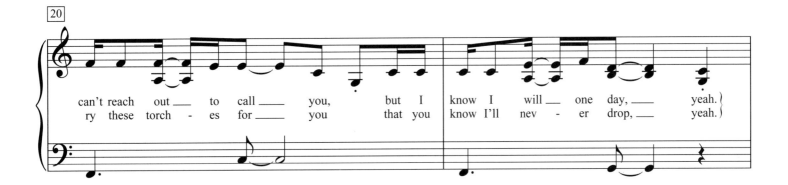

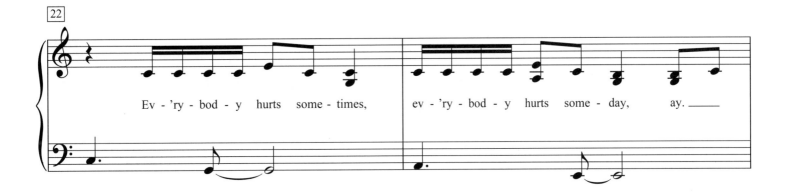

ev - 'ry - thing we've been through. Toast to the ones here to - day,

toast to the ones that we lost on the way. 'Cause the drinks bring back all the mem - o - ries and the

mem - o - ries bring back, mem-o-ries bring back you. Do do do do do do. Do do do — do do do do do.

Do do do — do do do do, mem-o-ries bring back, mem-o-ries bring back you. There's a

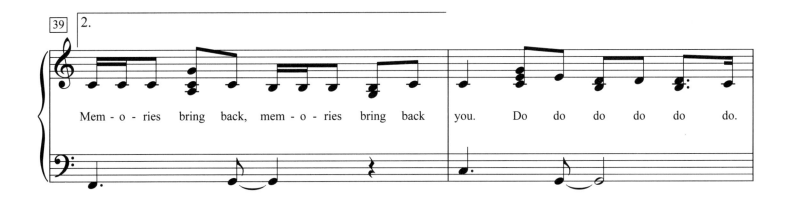

Mem - o - ries bring back, mem - o - ries bring back you. Do do do do do do.

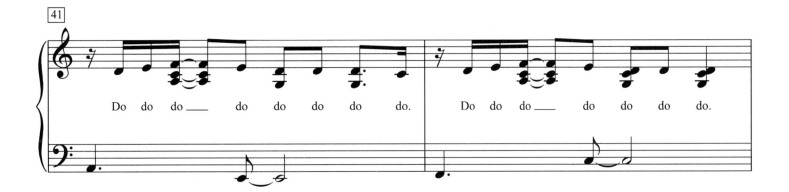

Do do do ____ do do do do do. Do do do ____ do do do do.

Mem - o - ries bring back, mem - o - ries bring back you. Yeah, yeah, yeah. ____ Yeah, yeah, yeah,

3

yeah, doh, doh. Mem - o - ries bring back, mem - o - ries bring back you.

No Time to Die

from NO TIME TO DIE

Words and Music by Billie Eilish O'Connell
and Finneas O'Connell
Arranged by Mona Rejino

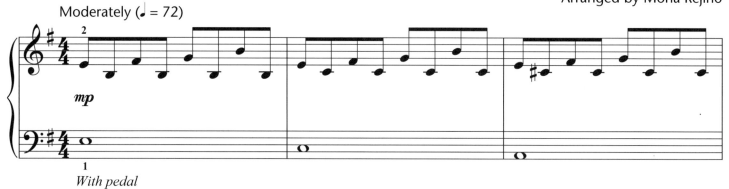

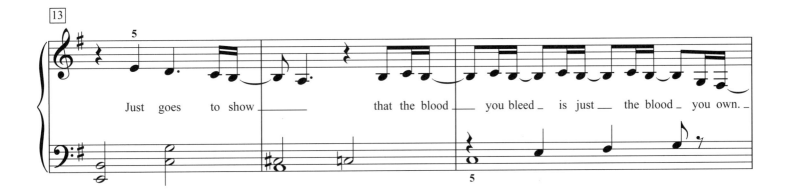

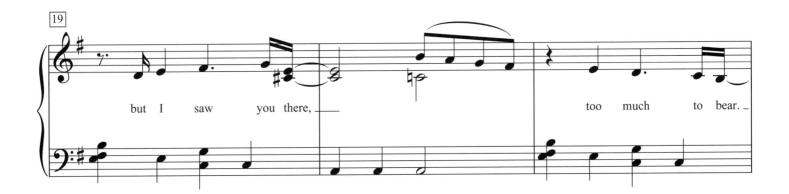

fair. Was I stu - pid to love __ you? Was I reck - less to help? __ Was it

ob - vi - ous __ to ev - 'ry bod - y else __ that I'd fall - en for __ a lie? __

You were nev - er on __ my side. __ Fool me once, __

___ fool me twice. __ Are you death __ or par - a - dise? __ Now you'll nev -

-er see me cry. There's just no time to die.

cresc. poco a poco

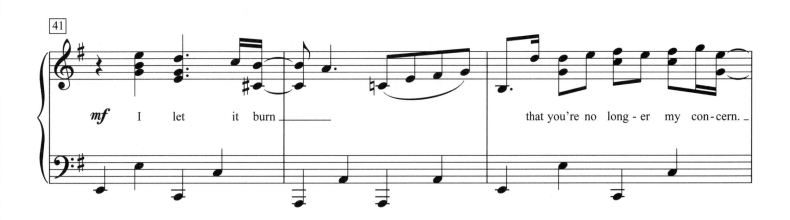

mf I let it burn that you're no long - er my con - cern.

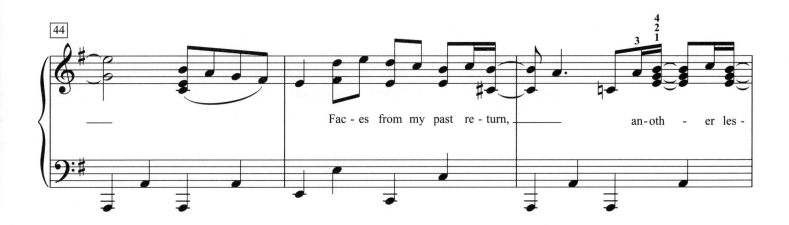

Fac - es from my past re - turn, an - oth - er les -

- son yet to learn, ___ that I'd fall - en for ___ a lie. ___

___ You were nev - er on ___ my side. ___ Fool me once, ___

___ fool me twice. ___ Are you death ___ or par - a - dise? ___ Now you'll nev -

- er see me cry. ___ There's just no time to die. ___

No time to die. _____ Mm. _____ No time to die. __

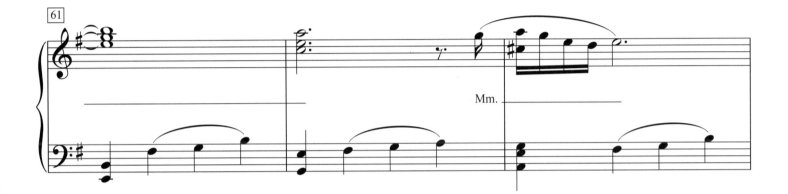

Mm.

Fool me once, _____ fool me twice. _ Are you death _____ or par - a - dise? Now you'll nev -

p

- er see me cry. ____ There's _ just no time to die. __

Señorita

Words and Music by Camila Cabello,
Charlotte Aitchison, Jack Patterson,
Shawn Mendes, Magnus Hoiberg,
Benjamin Levin, Ali Tamposi
and Andrew Wotman
Arranged by Mona Rejino

Moderate Latin groove (♩ = 116)

With pedal

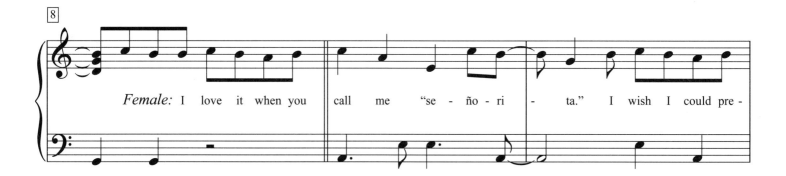

Female: I love it when you call me "se-ño-ri-ta." I wish I could pre-

tend I did-n't need ___ ya, but ev-'ry touch is ooh, la, ___ la, la. It's

true, la, ___ la, la. Ooh, ___ I should be run-nin'. Ooh, ___ you keep me com-in' for

Male:
ya. Land in Mi-am-i, the air was hot from sum-mer rain. Sweat drip-pin' off me.

Be-fore I e-ven knew her name, la, ___ la, la, it felt like

ooh, la, ___ la, la. Yeah, ___ no. ___ Sap-phire ___ moon-light,

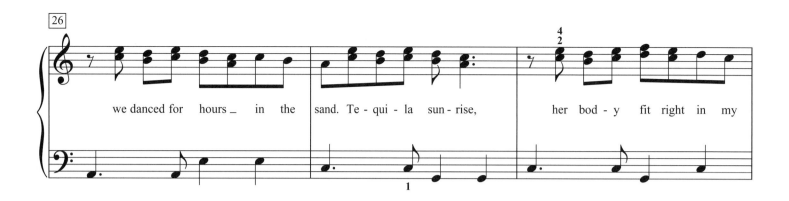

we danced for hours __ in the sand. Te - qui - la sun - rise, her bod - y fit right in my

hands, la, __ la, la. It felt like ooh, la, __ la, la, yeah. __ *Both:* I love it when you

call me "se - ño - ri - ta." I wish I could pre - tend I did - n't need __ ya, but ev -'ry touch is

ooh, la, __ la, la. It's true, la, __ la, la. Ooh, __ I should be run - nin'. Ooh, __

36

you know I love it when you call me "se - ño - ri - ta." I wish it was - n't

so damn hard to leave _____ ya, but ev -'ry touch is ooh, la, _____ la, la. It's

To Coda ⊕

true, la, _____ la, la. Ooh, _____ I should be run - nin'. Ooh, _____ you keep me com - in' for

Female:
ya. Locked in the ho - tel, there's just some things that nev - er change. You say we're just friends,

but friends don't know the way you taste, la, ___ la, la. 'Cause you

know it's been a long time com-in', don't you let me fall, oh. _____ Ooh, when _ your lips un-dress me,

D.S. al Coda

hooked on ___ your tongue. Ooh, love, _ your kiss is dead-ly. Don't stop. I love it when you

Both:
mf

CODA

ya. All a - long I'll ___ be com - in' ___ for ya. And I

hope it ___ meant some-thin' __ to ya. Call my name, I'll ___ be com-in' __ for

ya, com-in' __ for ya. *mp*

Ooh, _

___ I should be run-nin'. Ooh, ___ you keep me com-in' for ya.

Someone You Loved

Words and Music by Lewis Capaldi,
Benjamin Kohn, Peter Kelleher,
Thomas Barnes and Samuel Roman
Arranged by Mona Rejino

Moderate Ballad (♩ = 112)

With pedal

I'm go - ing un - der, and this time I fear there's no one to save me.
I'm go - ing un - der, and this time I fear there's no one to turn to.

This "all or noth - ing" real - ly got a way of driv - ing me cra -
This "all or noth - ing" way of lov - ing got me sleep - ing with - out

- zy. I need some-bod - y to heal, some-bod - y to know,
— you. I need some-bod - y to know, some-bod - y to heal,

some-bod - y to have, ____ some-bod - y to hold. ____ It's eas - y to say, ____
some-bod-y to have ____ just to know how it feels. ____ It's eas - y to say, ____

_____ but it's nev - er the same. ___ I guess I kind - a liked the way you numbed all the pain. ____
_____ but it's nev - er the same. ___ I guess I kind - a liked the way you helped me es - cape. ____

___ Now the day ___ bleeds ___ in - to night - fall, ____ and you're not here ____

mf

___ to get me through it all. I let my guard down, ____ and then you pulled the rug. ____

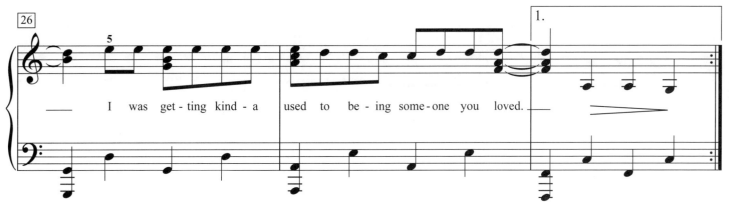

___ I was get - ting kind - a used to be - ing some - one you loved. ____

1.

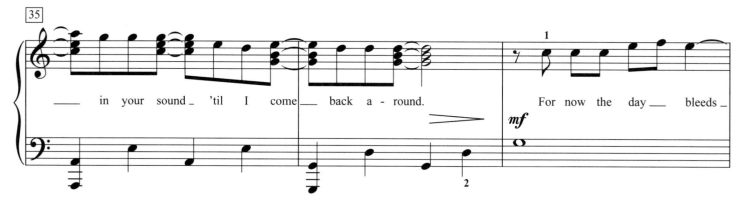

used to be - ing some-one you loved. ___ But now the day ___ bleeds ___ in - to night - fall, ___

mf

___ and you're not here ___ to get me through it all. I let my guard down, ___

___ and then you pulled the rug. ___ I was get - ting kind - a used to be - ing some-one you loved. ___

___ I let my guard down, ___ and then you pulled the rug. ___ I was get - ting kind - a

mp

used to be - ing some - one you loved. ___

poco rit.

Watermelon Sugar

Words and Music by Harry Styles,
Thomas Hull, Mitchell Rowland
and Tyler Johnson
Arranged by Mona Rejino

Moderate groove (♩ = 92)

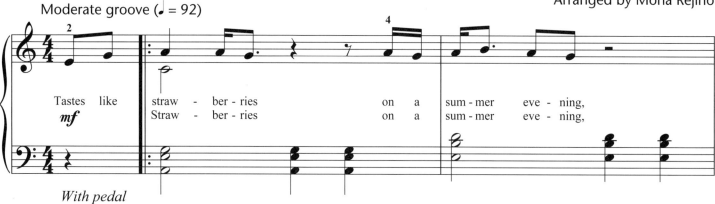

Tastes like straw - ber - ries on a sum - mer eve - ning,
Straw - ber - ries on a sum - mer eve - ning,

mf

With pedal

and it sounds just like a song. I want more ber - ries, and that
ba- by, you're the end of June. I want your bel - ly, and that

sum - mer feel - ing. It's so won - der - ful and warm. Breathe me in,
sum - mer feel - ing, get-ting washed a - way in you.

breathe me out. I don't know if I could ev - er go with-

out. I'm just think - ing out loud. I don't

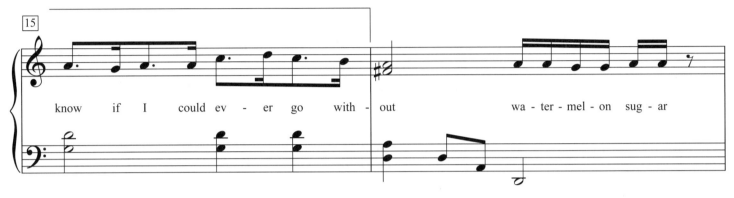

know if I could ev - er go with - out wa - ter - mel - on sug - ar

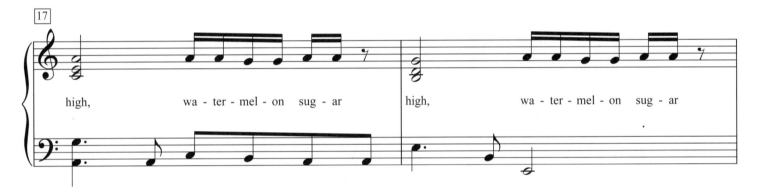

high, wa - ter - mel - on sug - ar high, wa - ter - mel - on sug - ar

high, wa - ter - mel - on sug - ar high. Wa - ter - mel - on sug - ar.

Wa - ter - mel - on sug - ar high, wa - ter - mel - on sug - ar

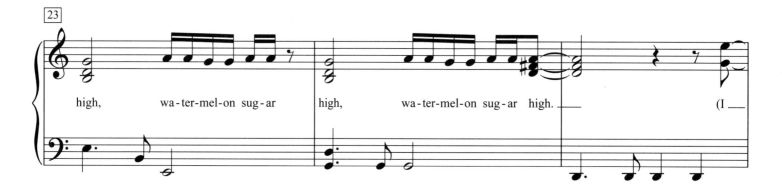

high, wa-ter-mel-on sug-ar high, wa-ter-mel-on sug-ar high. (I

just wan-na taste it, I just wan-na taste it, wa - ter-mel-on sug-ar high.)

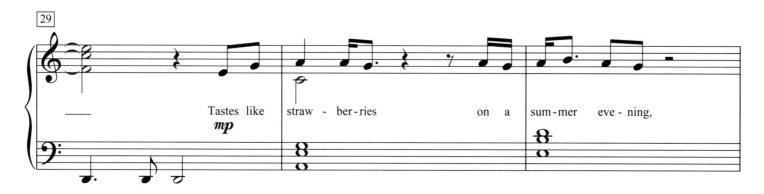

Tastes like straw-ber-ries on a sum-mer eve-ning,
mp

and it sounds just like a song. I want your bel-ly, and that

sum-mer feel-ing. I don't know if I could ev-er go with-out wa-ter-mel-on sug-ar
cresc.

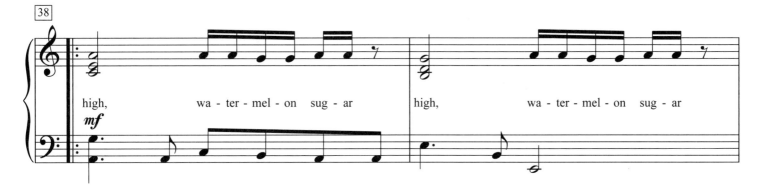

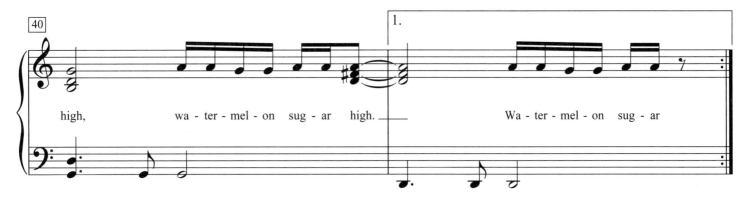

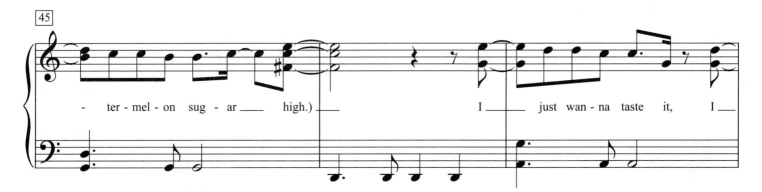

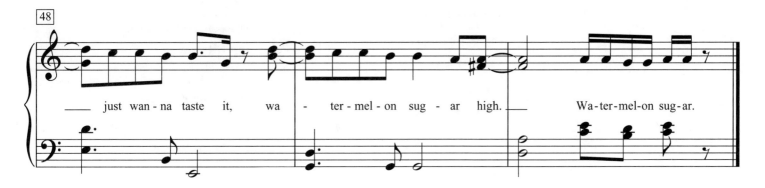

POPULAR SONGS

HAL LEONARD STUDENT PIANO LIBRARY

The **Hal Leonard Student Piano Library** has great songs, and you will find all your favorites here: Disney classics, Broadway and movie favorites, and today's top hits. These graded collections are skillfully and imaginatively arranged for students and pianists at every level, from elementary solos with teacher accompaniments to sophisticated piano solos for the advancing pianist.

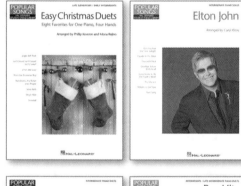

Adele
arr. Mona Rejino
00159590 Correlates with HLSPL Level 5..........$12.99

The Beatles
arr. Eugénie Rocherolle
00296649 Correlates with HLSPL Level 5..........$10.99

Irving Berlin Piano Duos
arr. Don Heitler and Jim Lyke
00296838 Correlates with HLSPL Level 5..........$14.99

Broadway Favorites
arr. Phillip Keveren
00279192 Correlates with HLSPL Level 4..........$12.99

Broadway Hits
arr. Carol Klose
00296650 Correlates with HLSPL Levels 4/5.......$8.99

Chart Hits
arr. Mona Rejino
00296710 Correlates with HLSPL Level 5............$8.99

Christmas Cheer
arr. Phillip Keveren
00296616 Correlates with HLSPL Level 4............$8.99

Classic Christmas Favorites
arr. Jennifer & Mike Watts
00129582 Correlates with HLSPL Level 5............$9.99

Christmas Time Is Here
arr. Eugénie Rocherolle
00296614 Correlates with HLSPL Level 5............$8.99

Classic Joplin Rags
arr. Fred Kern
00296743 Correlates with HLSPL Level 5............$9.99

Classical Pop –
Lady Gaga Fugue & Other Pop Hits
arr. Giovanni Dettori
00296921 Correlates with HLSPL Level 5..........$12.99

Contemporary Movie Hits
arr. by Carol Klose, Jennifer Linn and Wendy Stevens
00296780 Correlates with HLSPL Level 5............$8.99

Contemporary Pop Hits
arr. Wendy Stevens
00296836 Correlates with HLSPL Level 3............$8.99

Country Favorites
arr. Mona Rejino
00296861 Correlates with HLSPL Level 5............$9.99

Current Hits
arr. Mona Rejino
00296768 Correlates with HLSPL Level 5............$8.99

Disney Favorites
arr. Phillip Keveren
00296647 Correlates with HLSPL Levels 3/4.......$9.99

Disney Film Favorites
arr. Mona Rejino
00296809 Correlates with HLSPL Level 5..........$10.99

Easy Christmas Duets
arr. Mona Rejino and Phillip Keveren
00237139 Correlates with HLSPL Level 3/4........$9.99

Easy Disney Duets
arr. Jennifer and Mike Watts
00243727 Correlates with HLSPL Level 4..........$12.99

Four Hands on Broadway
arr. Fred Kern
00146177 Correlates with HLSPL Level 5..........$12.99

Jazz Hits for Piano Duet
arr. Jeremy Siskind
00143248 Correlates with HLSPL Level 5 ....$20.99

Elton John
arr. Carol Klose
00296721 Correlates with HLSPL Level 5............$8.99

Joplin Ragtime Duets
arr. Fred Kern
00296771 Correlates with HLSPL Level 5............$8.99

Jerome Kern Classics
arr. Eugénie Rocherolle
00296577 Correlates with HLSPL Level 5..........$12.99

Movie Blockbusters
arr. Mona Rejino
00232850 Correlates with HLSPL Level 5..........$10.99

Pop Hits for Piano Duet
arr. Jeremy Siskind
00224734 Correlates with HLSPL Level 5..........$12.99

Sing to the King
arr. Phillip Keveren
00296808 Correlates with HLSPL Level 5............$8.99

Smash Hits
arr. Mona Rejino
00284841 Correlates with HLSPL Level 5..........$10.99

Spooky Halloween Tunes
arr. Fred Kern
00121550 Correlates with HLSPL Levels 3/4.......$9.99

Today's Hits
arr. Mona Rejino
00296646 Correlates with HLSPL Level 5............$9.99

Top Hits
arr. Jennifer and Mike Watts
00296894 Correlates with HLSPL Level 5..........$10.99

Top Piano Ballads
arr. Jennifer Watts
00197926 Correlates with HLSPL Level 5..........$10.99

You Raise Me Up
arr. Deborah Brady
00296576 Correlates with HLSPL Levels 2/3.......$7.95

HAL•LEONARD®

7777 W. BLUEMOUND RD. P.O. BOX 13819 MILWAUKEE, WI 53213

Visit our website at **www.halleonard.com**

Prices, contents and availability subject to change without notice. Prices may vary outside the U.S.